BEAT ANXIETY NOW

Practical Tips to Calm Your Mind and Find Peace in a Busy World

Cynthia David

COPYRIGHT

CONTENTS

INTRODUCTION

Anxiety is something I've dealt with for as long as I can remember. For years, I brushed off the sleepless nights, the constant worrying, and the pounding heart as "just stress." But as time went on, it became harder to ignore. I found myself constantly on edge, overthinking every little thing, and struggling to stay present in the moment. It wasn't until anxiety started affecting my relationships, my work, and my overall well-being that I realized I needed to do something about it.

I've also watched people I care about deeply suffer from anxiety. Friends and family who, on the outside, appeared to have it all together, were silently battling inner chaos. One close friend, who was always the life of the party, confided in me one day about the overwhelming panic attacks she'd been having. She felt ashamed, thinking she was the only one struggling. That moment opened my eyes to how many of us are quietly fighting the same battle, feeling isolated and helpless.

I wrote this book because I know how crippling anxiety can be, and I also know that it doesn't have to control your life. Over the years, I've discovered tools and strategies that have helped me find calm in the midst of chaos. These are real, practical steps that anyone can follow, no matter how overwhelming life feels right now. And that's the heart of this book – to offer guidance that is simple, straightforward, and effective.

Anxiety, at its core, is our body's natural response to stress. It's that feeling of worry, nervousness, or unease about something that's uncertain or out of our control. In small doses, anxiety can be helpful – it keeps us alert and aware of potential dangers. But when anxiety becomes constant or overwhelming, it can interfere with our daily lives.

In today's fast-paced world, anxiety has become all too common. We're juggling endless to-do lists, dealing with information overload, and navigating a society that often values productivity over well-being. Social media, while connecting us, can also fuel feelings of inadequacy and comparison. All of this contributes to why so many people feel anxious, stressed, or just "off" much of the time.

But here's the good news: anxiety doesn't have to run your life. It's possible to find peace, even in the middle of a busy, hectic world. And this book is here to show you how.

The Purpose of This Book

The purpose of this book is simple: to help you calm your mind and reclaim your peace, no matter how busy or stressed you feel. I won't be giving you vague advice or telling you to "just relax." Instead, I'll share practical, down-to-earth tips that you can start using right away to reduce your anxiety. These are techniques I've personally used and seen work for others – from quick fixes you can try in moments of panic, to long-term strategies for managing anxiety over time.

You don't need to have hours of free time or be a meditation expert to benefit from this book. Whether you're a working professional, a parent, a student, or someone juggling it all, these tips are designed to fit into your life as it is right now.

A Promise of Peace

I understand that when you're deep in anxiety, it can feel like there's no way out. But I'm here to remind you that peace is possible, and it's closer than you think. The techniques in this book aren't magic fixes – they require practice and patience. But I promise you that if you commit to trying them, you will begin to notice a shift.

You deserve to feel calm. You deserve to have peace of mind. And through the pages of this book,

I'll walk with you step by step, showing you that no matter how busy or stressed you feel, you can find the stillness you've been searching for.

This is your journey to a calmer, more peaceful life. Let's take the first step together.

"You are stronger than your anxiety. Take things one step at a time, and you'll find your way to peace."

CHAPTER 1

Understanding Anxiety – What It Is and Why It Happens

Anxiety is a feeling we've all experienced at some point in our lives. It's that knot in your stomach before a big exam, the racing heart before a job interview, or the unease you feel when facing an uncertain situation. In small amounts, anxiety can be a good thing – it keeps us alert and ready to respond to challenges. But when anxiety becomes overwhelming and constant, it can feel like it's taking over your life.

So, what exactly is anxiety, and why does it happen? Let's break it down in simple terms.

What Is Anxiety?

Anxiety is our body's natural response to stress. It's a mental and physical reaction to perceived threats or danger. Imagine anxiety as your body's internal alarm system – when you sense something threatening, your brain sends out signals to get you ready to deal with it.

But here's the thing: sometimes that alarm goes off even when there's no real danger. **For example**, you might feel anxious about making a mistake at work or meeting new people, even though these situations aren't life-threatening. Your brain, however, doesn't always know the difference between a real threat and a perceived one. This is why you can feel intense anxiety even when logically you know there's no immediate danger.

When you feel anxious, your body goes through a series of changes. You might notice your heart beating faster, your palms getting sweaty, or your breathing becoming shallow. These physical responses are part of what's known as the **fight-or-flight response** – your body's way of preparing to either confront or escape from a threat.

Here's what happens behind the scenes: when you feel anxious, your brain triggers the release of certain chemicals like **adrenaline** and **cortisol**. These are stress hormones that flood your body, giving you a burst of energy and making you more alert. Your heart pumps more blood, your muscles tense up, and your senses become sharper. This is great if you're in a dangerous situation, like avoiding a car accident. But when this happens too often, or in situations where there's no real danger, it can take a toll on your body and mind.

Why Some Anxiety Is Normal, but Too Much Is Overwhelming

It's important to understand that some anxiety is normal. In fact, anxiety has been crucial to our survival as a species. Thousands of years ago, our ancestors needed to react quickly to dangers like predators or hostile environments. Their anxiety helped them stay alert and alive.

Today, we don't face the same life-or-death threats, but our bodies haven't fully adapted to modern stressors. Everyday situations like work pressure, social interactions, or financial worries can still trigger that ancient fight-or-flight response. In small doses, this anxiety can help motivate you to perform well under pressure or stay safe in risky situations.

However, when anxiety becomes constant or overwhelming, it stops being helpful. Instead of just preparing you for action, it starts interfering with your life. You might feel on edge all the time, unable to relax even when there's no immediate stress. This is when anxiety moves from being a normal reaction to a problem that needs to be addressed.

Different Types of Anxiety

Not all anxiety is the same. There are different types of anxiety disorders that people can experience, each with its own set of challenges.

Here's a simple overview of some common types of anxiety:

- **Generalized Anxiety Disorder (GAD)**: This is when you feel anxious most of the time, even when there's no clear reason. People with GAD often worry about everyday things like work, health, or relationships, and find it hard to control their worrying.

- **Social Anxiety Disorder**: Social anxiety is an intense fear of being judged or embarrassed in social situations. People with this type of anxiety may avoid social gatherings, public speaking, or even small group settings because they fear being scrutinized or humiliated.

- **Panic Disorder**: Panic disorder is marked by sudden, intense episodes of fear known as panic attacks. During a panic attack, you might feel like you're losing control, having a heart attack, or even dying. These attacks can happen without warning and often lead to a fear of having more panic attacks.

- **Phobias**: A phobia is an irrational fear of a specific object, situation, or activity. Common phobias include fear of heights, flying, spiders, or crowded spaces. Even though the fear may be out of proportion to the actual danger, it can feel very real and overwhelming.

- **Obsessive-Compulsive Disorder (OCD)**: OCD involves unwanted, persistent thoughts (obsessions) and repetitive behaviors (compulsions). For example, someone with OCD might feel the need to check the locks on their doors multiple times or wash their hands repeatedly to relieve anxiety.

- **Post-Traumatic Stress Disorder (PTSD)**: PTSD can develop after experiencing a traumatic event. People with PTSD may have flashbacks, nightmares, or severe anxiety related to the trauma, and they may avoid places or situations that remind them of it.

While anxiety can feel overpowering, the good news is that it's something that can be managed. By understanding what anxiety is and why it happens, you've already taken the first step toward regaining control. In the next chapters, I'll dive into practical techniques and strategies to help you calm your mind, reduce anxiety, and find peace, even in the middle of life's chaos.

Remember, anxiety doesn't define you. It's a natural response, but it doesn't have to rule your life. You have the power to change your relationship with anxiety, and this book will guide you on that journey.

Let's take the next step together.

"Don't let anxiety stop you from living fully. Every day is an opportunity to rise above it."

CHAPTER 2

Identifying Your Anxiety Triggers

If you're reading this book, chances are you've experienced anxiety at some point, but have you ever stopped to ask yourself what's really causing it? Understanding what triggers your anxiety is a key step toward managing it. By identifying your specific triggers, you can start making changes in how you respond to them, reducing their impact on your life.

This chapter will guide you through practical steps to help you figure out what's causing your anxiety. You'll also learn how to spot the signs of anxiety and how to keep track of your triggers in an anxiety journal.

What Are Anxiety Triggers?

Anxiety triggers are situations, thoughts, or events that spark feelings of fear, worry, or nervousness. These triggers can vary from person to person – what makes one person anxious may not affect someone else at all. Common anxiety triggers include work deadlines, relationship issues, financial stress, health concerns, and even certain social settings. But triggers can also be less obvious, like specific thoughts or memories that bring up feelings of fear or discomfort.

Identifying your anxiety triggers helps you gain control over how you react to them. When you know what's setting off your anxiety, you can prepare yourself and use techniques to manage it.

Spotting the Signs of Anxiety

Before diving into how to identify your triggers, it's important to recognize the physical, emotional, and mental signs of anxiety. These signs can vary, but here are some common ones to look out for:

Physical Signs:

- Rapid heartbeat or chest tightness
- Shallow or fast breathing
- Sweaty palms or cold hands
- Headaches or dizziness
- Stomach issues like nausea or a "knot" in your stomach
- Muscle tension or shaking

Emotional Signs:

- Feeling irritable or restless

- A sense of dread or overwhelming fear

- Trouble focusing on anything but your worries

- Feeling detached from reality or people around you (like you're in a dream)

- Difficulty relaxing, even in calm situations

Mental Signs:

- Overthinking or ruminating on worst-case scenarios

- Constantly worrying about future events or things you can't control

- Feeling like your mind is racing and you can't slow it down

- Trouble concentrating or remembering things because your mind is preoccupied with worries

Recognizing these signs is the first step in understanding when your anxiety is being triggered. Once you know how anxiety shows up in your body and mind, you can begin to link these reactions to specific triggers.

Practical Steps to Identify Your Triggers

Now that you know how anxiety feels, let's move on to figuring out what's causing it. Here are some practical steps you can follow:

1. Start Noticing Patterns

Think about the times when your anxiety has been the most intense. Was there a common situation, person, or event that triggered it? It could be a specific place (like crowded stores), a recurring situation (like meetings at work), or even certain thoughts (like fear of failure).

2. Pay Attention to Your Body

Your body often reacts to anxiety before your mind does. When you start to feel anxious, notice what's happening in your body. Is your heart racing? Are your palms sweating? Are your muscles tense? Physical symptoms can be a clue that something in your environment is triggering your anxiety.

3. Reflect on Your Thoughts

Your thoughts play a big role in triggering anxiety. Sometimes anxiety is triggered by negative thought patterns, like assuming the worst or feeling out of control. Ask yourself: What was I thinking about when I started feeling anxious? Were my thoughts realistic, or was I jumping to conclusions?

4. Look at Your Environment

Your surroundings can also influence your anxiety. Are there certain places that make you feel more stressed? Is there a particular person or group of people who heighten your anxiety? Your environment, both physical and social, can have a big impact on how you feel.

Take some time to reflect on the following questions. Write down your answers to gain clarity on what might be triggering your anxiety.

1. **What situations usually make me feel anxious?**

   (Examples: giving presentations, meeting new people, dealing with conflict)

2. **Are there specific people who increase my anxiety?**

   (Examples: a boss, a family member, a social group)

3. **What thoughts or fears often run through my mind when I feel anxious?**

(Examples: fear of failure, worry about the future, thoughts of being judged)

4. **What physical signs do I notice when my anxiety is triggered?**

(Examples: heart racing, sweating, feeling shaky)

5. **Are there patterns or common themes in what makes me anxious?**

(Examples: deadlines at work, health concerns, financial worries)

By answering these questions, you'll start to see patterns in your anxiety. Identifying your biggest stressors is the first step in taking back control.

Keeping an Anxiety Journal

One of the most effective tools for identifying and managing your anxiety is keeping a journal. An anxiety journal helps you track when and where your anxiety shows up, what triggers it, and how you respond. It also helps you notice patterns over time, which is key to understanding your anxiety better.

Here's how to get started:

1. **Write Down Your Anxiety Episodes**: Whenever you feel anxious, jot down the time, date, and what was happening when the anxiety started. Be as specific as possible about the situation.

2. **Note Your Physical and Emotional Symptoms**: Record how your body reacted and

what emotions you felt. Did your heart race? Were you sweating or shaking? Were you feeling fearful or overwhelmed?

3. **Identify the Trigger**: Reflect on what might have triggered your anxiety in that moment. Was it a specific event, thought, or person? Even if the trigger isn't clear right away, write down any clues you can think of.

4. **Record Your Response**: How did you deal with the anxiety? Did you leave the situation, try deep breathing, or simply push through it? Noting your response will help you see what works for you and what doesn't.

5. **Look for Patterns**: After keeping the journal for a few weeks, review your entries. Do you notice any common triggers? Are there certain times of day or specific situations where your anxiety is worse? Spotting these patterns can help you

prepare for future anxiety episodes and develop better coping strategies.

By identifying your triggers and understanding how anxiety affects your body and mind, you've taken a huge step toward managing it. This chapter has equipped you with tools to recognize when and why your anxiety is being triggered, and how to track it through self-reflection and journaling. As you move forward, you'll be able to use this awareness to minimize the impact of anxiety on your daily life.

Remember, anxiety may show up uninvited, but with the right knowledge and tools, you can reduce its power over you. Keep going – you're on the path to understanding and managing your anxiety, one trigger at a time.

CHAPTER 3

Quick Fixes for Calming Anxiety in the Moment

Anxiety can strike at any time, whether you're sitting at your desk, standing in line, or even in the comfort of your own home. When it does, you need something quick and effective to help calm your mind and body before things get overwhelming. This chapter covers practical, easy-to-use techniques that you can use anytime anxiety starts creeping in.

These simple strategies won't solve the underlying causes of anxiety (we'll get to that in later chapters), but they will give you quick relief in the moment, allowing you to regain control when anxiety feels overpowering.

Breathing Techniques: Instantly Reduce Stress

When you're feeling anxious, your body often responds with shallow, rapid breathing. This only makes the anxiety worse by sending a signal to your brain that something is wrong. One of the quickest ways to calm yourself is by focusing on your breath and changing the way you breathe.

1. 4-7-8 Breathing Technique

This simple breathing exercise can help lower your stress levels in just a few minutes. It forces your body to slow down and encourages deeper, more relaxing breaths. Here's how to do it:

1. Sit comfortably, with your back straight and your feet on the ground.

2. Close your eyes and inhale deeply through your nose for a count of 4.

3. Hold your breath for a count of 7.

4. Exhale slowly through your mouth for a count of 8.

5. Repeat this cycle 4-5 times, focusing on the rhythm of your breath.

This technique works by slowing your heart rate and promoting a state of relaxation. It's great for when you need to calm down fast, whether you're about to give a presentation, sitting in traffic, or just feeling overwhelmed.

2. Box Breathing (Square Breathing)

This exercise is another simple but powerful way to bring your breathing under control and calm your mind. It's especially helpful when you feel like your thoughts are racing or you can't focus.

1. Inhale slowly through your nose for a count of 4.
2. Hold your breath for a count of 4.
3. Exhale through your mouth for a count of 4.
4. Hold your breath again for a count of 4.
5. Repeat the cycle several times, keeping the breaths slow and steady.

The rhythm of this technique helps balance your nervous system and refocuses your mind, making it easier to manage anxious thoughts.

Grounding Exercises: Bringing Yourself Back to the Present

When anxiety takes over, it often pulls you out of the present moment and makes you worry about the future or dwell on the past. Grounding exercises are designed to help you reconnect with the present by using your senses—sight, sound, touch, taste, and smell.

1. The 5-4-3-2-1 Grounding Technique

This exercise uses your senses to bring your mind back to the present moment and interrupt anxious thoughts. Here's how to do it:

1. **Look** around and name **5 things** you can see.

2. **Touch** 4 things around you. Focus on their texture and how they feel.

3. **Listen** and identify 3 sounds you can hear.

4. **Smell** 2 things (if nothing is nearby, take a deep breath and imagine a familiar scent).

5. **Taste** 1 thing, even if it's just the taste of your mouth.

This technique helps you ground yourself by shifting your attention away from anxious thoughts and back to your immediate surroundings. It's a simple but powerful way to break the cycle of anxiety.

2. Grounding Through Touch

Another quick grounding exercise involves using touch to bring your awareness back to the present.

When you're feeling anxious, find a small object (a keychain, a smooth stone, or even your clothing) and hold it in your hands. Focus on its texture—how does it feel against your skin? Is it rough or smooth? Warm or cool?

This simple act of focusing on something tangible can help disrupt anxious thought patterns and remind your brain that you're safe in the present moment.

Physical Movement: Release Tension and Calm Your Mind

When anxiety strikes, your body often holds tension in different areas, like your shoulders, neck, and chest. Gentle physical movement can help release this tension, allowing your body to relax and your mind to follow.

1. Shoulder Shrugs and Rls

Tension often builds up in your shoulders, especially when you're feeling anxious. Here's a quick way to release it:

1. Take a deep breath in and raise your shoulders up toward your ears, holding them there for a moment.

2. Exhale slowly and drop your shoulders down.

3. Roll your shoulders in slow circles, first forward, then backward.

This movement helps loosen up tight muscles and reduces the physical discomfort that can come with anxiety.

2. Stretching Your Neck

Anxiety can cause tightness in your neck, which leads to headaches and more stress. Here's a simple stretch you can do anywhere:

1. Sit or stand up straight, with your shoulders relaxed.

2. Slowly tilt your head to one side, bringing your ear toward your shoulder. Hold for 15-20 seconds.

3. Switch sides and repeat.

This stretch helps release tension in your neck and shoulders, promoting relaxation throughout your body.

3. Taking a Short Walk

Sometimes, the best way to deal with anxiety is to change your environment, even if it's just for a few minutes. A quick walk outside, around your office, or in your home can help calm your mind and reduce the intensity of your anxiety. Physical movement encourages the release of endorphins, which are your body's natural "feel-good" chemicals. Plus, being outside can give you a mental break and allow you to return to your task feeling more focused and calm.

Visualization: Creating Mental "Safe Spaces"

Visualization is a powerful tool that allows you to create a mental escape when you're feeling overwhelmed by anxiety. By picturing yourself in a calm, peaceful place, you can trick your brain into feeling more relaxed.

1. Safe Space Visualization

Here's how to create your own mental "safe space":

1. Close your eyes and take a few deep breaths.

2. Picture a place where you feel completely safe and relaxed. It could be a real place you've been to (a beach, a forest, a favorite room), or it could be an imaginary place.

3. Focus on the details of that place. What do you see? What do you hear? Can you feel the warmth of the sun or a cool breeze on your skin? The more details you imagine, the more real it will feel.

4. Spend a few minutes in this mental safe space, allowing the calmness of the scene to wash over you.

When you return to the present moment, you'll likely feel more grounded and peaceful. This technique is especially useful when you can't physically leave a stressful situation, but you still need a mental break.

2. Visualizing Your Anxiety Floating Away

Here's another simple visualization to try when you're feeling anxious:

1. Close your eyes and imagine your anxiety as a physical object, like a dark cloud or a heavy weight.

2. Picture that object slowly floating away from you. It could rise up into the sky or drift away on a river.

3. As the object moves farther away, notice how your body feels lighter and your mind feels clearer.

This visualization helps you mentally detach from your anxiety, giving you a sense of relief and control.

In this chapter, you've learned several quick and effective techniques for calming anxiety in the moment. Whether it's breathing exercises, grounding techniques, physical movement, or visualization, these tools are designed to help you regain control when anxiety strikes.

Remember, the goal of these exercises isn't to completely eliminate anxiety (it's a natural part of life), but to manage it in a way that keeps you calm and in control. With practice, these techniques will become second nature, giving you the power to calm your mind and find peace no matter how busy or stressful your day may be.

"Anxiety might show up uninvited, but it doesn't have to stay. You control the door."

CHAPTER 4

Building Long-Term Strategies to Manage Anxiety

Quick fixes can help you calm down in the moment, but managing anxiety in the long term requires building healthy habits. By incorporating daily routines that support your mental and physical well-being, you can prevent anxiety from taking over your life. This chapter looks at practical strategies you can start using today—simple lifestyle changes that can significantly reduce anxiety over time.

The Importance of Daily Routines

When life feels chaotic, it's easy for anxiety to creep in. Establishing a consistent daily routine can bring a sense of order and predictability, which is crucial for calming the mind. Knowing what to expect from your day can reduce stress, making it easier to cope with unexpected challenges.

Here are some key components of a routine that can help keep anxiety in check:

- **Start your day with intention**: Instead of rushing into the day, take a few minutes in the morning to center yourself. Whether it's through stretching, meditation, or simply sitting quietly with a cup of tea, starting your day calmly sets the tone for how you'll handle stress.

- **Prioritize self-care**: Make sure your routine includes time for self-care activities—whether it's exercise, reading, or enjoying a hobby. These moments of self-nurturing keep your mental and emotional balance in check.

- **Create structure in your workday**: Break your tasks into manageable steps, and schedule regular breaks. A packed schedule can make you feel overwhelmed, but organizing your day into focused work periods and short breaks helps keep anxiety at bay.

Exercise: How Moving Your Body Reduces Anxiety

Exercise is one of the most effective natural remedies for anxiety. Physical activity helps reduce the body's stress hormones, like adrenaline and cortisol, while boosting endorphins—chemicals in the brain that improve mood and promote relaxation.

You don't need to become a marathon runner to see the benefits. Even small amounts of regular exercise can make a big difference.

How Exercise Helps:

- **Reduces Tension**: Physical activity relaxes tight muscles and helps the body release built-up tension.

- **Boosts Mood**: Exercise increases the production of neurotransmitters like serotonin and dopamine, which are known to improve mood and reduce feelings of anxiety.

- **Improves Sleep**: People who exercise regularly tend to sleep better, which plays a big role in managing anxiety.

Simple Ways to Add Movement to Your Day:

- **Take short walks**: A brisk 10-15 minute walk, even around your neighborhood or during lunch breaks, can help clear your mind and lower anxiety.

- **Try stretching**: Gentle stretches or yoga can release tension and bring your focus to your body, rather than your anxious thoughts.

- **Join an activity you enjoy**: Whether it's dancing, swimming, or even gardening, doing something you love keeps you moving and engaged, without feeling like a chore.

Sleep: The Impact of Rest on Anxiety

Sleep and anxiety are deeply connected. When you're anxious, it can be hard to sleep, and a lack of sleep can make your anxiety worse. Getting enough rest is one of the most important things you can do for your mental health.

Why Sleep Matters for Anxiety:

- **Restores the brain**: While you sleep, your brain processes emotions and resets your stress response system. Without proper sleep, your ability to handle stress decreases.

- **Regulates mood**: Poor sleep leads to irritability and makes it harder to think clearly or make decisions. This can trigger anxious feelings.

- **Strengthens resilience**: A well-rested mind is better equipped to deal with daily challenges, preventing anxiety from spiraling out of control.

Tips for Better Sleep:

- **Stick to a sleep schedule**: Go to bed and wake up at the same time every day, even on weekends. Consistency helps regulate your body's internal clock.

- **Create a relaxing bedtime routine**: Develop a wind-down routine that signals to your body it's time for rest. This might include dimming the lights, reading, or taking a warm bath.

- **Limit screen time before bed**: The blue light from phones and computers can interfere with your body's production of melatonin, the hormone that helps you sleep. Try to unplug at least an hour before bed.

Diet: Foods That Help (and Hurt) Your Anxiety Levels

What you eat has a direct impact on how you feel—physically and mentally. Certain foods can fuel anxiety, while others can help calm your nervous system and keep stress in check.

Foods That Help Reduce Anxiety:

- **Leafy greens** (like spinach and kale): These are rich in magnesium, which helps regulate the stress response.

- **Omega-3 rich foods** (like salmon, walnuts, and flaxseeds): Omega-3 fatty acids are known to reduce inflammation and support brain health, which can lower anxiety.

- **Whole grains** (like oats, quinoa, and brown rice): These foods provide steady energy and help keep blood sugar levels stable, preventing mood swings and irritability.

- **Probiotic-rich foods** (like yogurt, kefir, and kimchi): Gut health is closely linked to mental health. Foods rich in probiotics can help improve your mood and reduce anxiety.

Foods to Avoid or Limit:

- **Caffeine**: While a cup of coffee might help wake you up, too much caffeine can increase heart rate, make you jittery, and trigger anxious feelings.

- **Sugar**: Sugary snacks or drinks cause blood sugar levels to spike and crash, which can lead to mood swings and increased anxiety.

- **Processed foods**: Highly processed foods, like fast food or chips, lack the nutrients your brain needs to function properly and can contribute to feelings of anxiety.

Mindfulness and Meditation: Simple Practices for Lasting Peace

Mindfulness is about staying present in the moment rather than worrying about the future or ruminating on the past. Meditation is a tool that helps you practice mindfulness, making it easier to let go of anxious thoughts and find calm.

The Benefits of Mindfulness:

- **Reduces negative thinking**: By focusing on the present, mindfulness helps prevent anxious thoughts from spiraling out of control.

- **Improves emotional regulation**: When you practice mindfulness, you become more aware of your emotions and better able to manage them.

- **Promotes relaxation**: Mindfulness encourages deep breathing and relaxation, helping you stay calm even in stressful situations.

Easy Ways to Practice Mindfulness and Meditation:

- **Start small**: You don't need to meditate for hours to see benefits. Just a few minutes of focused breathing can make a difference. Find a quiet spot, close your eyes, and focus on your breath.

- **Body scan meditation**: Lie down or sit comfortably. Starting from your toes, slowly focus on each part of your body, noticing any tension or sensations. As you move up, release tension from each area.

- **Mindful breathing**: Simply focus on your breath—how it feels as you inhale and exhale. When your mind wanders (and it will), gently bring it back to your breath without judgment.

Building long-term strategies to manage anxiety takes time and practice, but the rewards are worth it. By incorporating these routines—exercise, proper sleep, a balanced diet, and mindfulness—you can create a lifestyle that supports your mental health and keeps anxiety at bay.

Remember, anxiety doesn't have to control your life. With these daily habits, you're building a foundation for calm and resilience, giving yourself the tools to handle whatever challenges come your way.

"Small daily actions can create
big changes. Be patient with
yourself, and keep practicing
calm."

CHAPTER 5

Managing Anxiety at Work and in Social Situations

Work and social situations are some of the most common sources of anxiety for many people. The pressure to meet deadlines, perform well, and navigate interactions with others can easily trigger stress. Learning how to manage anxiety in these environments is crucial for your mental well-being and overall happiness. In this chapter, I'll explore practical strategies for handling work-related stress, avoiding burnout, setting boundaries, and managing social anxiety.

The demands of the workplace can often feel overwhelming. Long hours, heavy workloads, and constant pressure can make it hard to keep anxiety under control. Burnout happens when you're constantly stressed at work and start feeling exhausted, unmotivated, and disconnected from your tasks.

Recognizing the Signs of Work-Related Anxiety

- **Feeling overwhelmed by tasks**: If you're constantly feeling like there's too much to do and not enough time, this can lead to anxiety.

- **Perfectionism**: Trying to do everything perfectly can create unrealistic expectations and cause stress.

- **Irritability or frustration**: Constant stress can make you feel more on edge and easily annoyed by coworkers or work-related challenges.

Practical Tips for Managing Work Stress

- **Prioritize tasks**: Focus on the most important tasks first, and break big projects into smaller, manageable steps. This will make your workload feel less overwhelming.

- **Take regular breaks**: Step away from your desk for short breaks throughout the day. Even a five-minute walk or a quick stretch can help clear your mind and reduce anxiety.

- **Avoid multitasking**: Multitasking can increase stress because your brain is constantly switching between tasks. Try to focus on one thing at a time for better results and less anxiety.

Avoiding Burnout

- **Set boundaries**: It's important to know your limits. Don't take on more than you can handle, and learn to say no when your plate is full (more on this below).

- **Make time for self-care**: Outside of work, prioritize activities that help you relax and recharge. Whether it's spending time with loved ones, exercising, or pursuing hobbies, self-care is essential to avoid burnout.

Tips for Setting Boundaries and Saying "No" Without Guilt

One of the main reasons people feel overwhelmed and anxious at work or in social situations is because they take on too much. Setting boundaries is key to protecting your mental health, but many people struggle with saying "no" because they fear disappointing others or feeling guilty.

Setting boundaries allows you to protect your time and energy. Without them, you may find yourself stretched too thin, trying to please everyone but ending up exhausted and anxious.

How to Say "No" Without Guilt

- **Be direct but polite**: When saying no, it's important to be clear and respectful. You can say something like, "I appreciate the opportunity, but I'm unable to take on any more tasks at the moment."

- **Offer an alternative**: If saying no feels difficult, you can offer a compromise. For example, "I can't take on that project right now, but I can help next week."

- **Understand your limits**: Knowing your own limits is key to setting boundaries. You're not being selfish by saying no; you're protecting your mental and emotional well-being.

Staying Calm During Presentations, Meetings, and Deadlines

Work situations like presentations, meetings, and tight deadlines can trigger anxiety in many people. The fear of making mistakes or being judged by others can feel overwhelming. Fortunately, there are strategies you can use to stay calm and confident.

Preparing for Presentations and Meetings

- **Practice**: Rehearsing your presentation or points for a meeting can help you feel more confident and prepared. The more familiar you are with the material, the less anxiety you'll feel.

- **Breathe**: Before speaking, take a few deep breaths to calm your nerves. Slow, deep breathing helps lower your heart rate and reduce feelings of panic.

- **Visualize success**: Imagine yourself delivering a successful presentation or contributing to a meeting with ease.

Visualization can help shift your mindset and reduce anxiety.

Managing Deadlines

- **Break tasks into smaller steps**: When faced with a looming deadline, break the project into smaller tasks and focus on completing one step at a time. This prevents the project from feeling overwhelming.

- **Ask for help if needed**: If you're struggling to meet a deadline, don't be afraid to ask for help or delegate tasks. It's better to seek support than to push yourself to the point of burnout.

- **Stay organized**: Use a to-do list or project management tool to keep track of tasks and deadlines. Organization reduces the chance of last-minute panic.

Social anxiety can make gatherings, parties, or events feel stressful and uncomfortable. Whether it's the fear of being judged, feeling out of place, or struggling with small talk, social situations can be a major source of anxiety for many people.

Recognizing Social Anxiety

- **Fear of judgment**: You may worry excessively about what others think of you or fear that you'll say something embarrassing.

- **Avoiding social situations**: Social anxiety can lead you to avoid gatherings, meetings, or even casual hangouts to avoid the discomfort.

- **Physical symptoms**: Social anxiety often comes with physical symptoms like a racing heart, sweating, or feeling shaky.

Tips for Managing Social Anxiety at Events

- **Prepare conversation starters**: Before going to a social event, think of a few simple conversation starters to break the ice. Questions like "How do you know the host?" or "Have you tried the food?" can help ease the tension.

- **Practice mindfulness**: If you feel anxiety rising, focus on your breathing or use a grounding technique, such as feeling the texture of your clothes or noticing the sounds around you. This can help bring you back to the present moment.

- **Set small goals**: If social events feel overwhelming, set small, manageable goals for yourself, such as talking to one new person or staying for a specific amount of time. You don't need to stay at the event for hours—just focus on making progress.

Leaving Without Guilt

If a social situation becomes too overwhelming, it's okay to leave early. Give yourself permission to prioritize your mental health. A polite exit, such as thanking the host and saying you need to leave, is perfectly acceptable.

Anxiety in work and social settings is common, but it doesn't have to control your life. By using these strategies—setting boundaries, preparing for stressful situations, and practicing mindfulness—you can reduce your anxiety and approach work and social events with greater confidence.

Remember, managing anxiety is about finding what works for you. These tips are here to help guide you, but don't be afraid to experiment with different approaches until you find the strategies that make you feel most at ease. With practice, you can handle any work or social situation without letting anxiety take over.

CHAPTER 6

The Power of Positive Thinking and Gratitude

Our thoughts have a powerful impact on how we feel. Anxiety often comes from negative thinking—worrying about what could go wrong, doubting yourself, or imagining worst-case scenarios. But just as negative thinking can fuel anxiety, positive thinking can calm it. This chapter explores how changing your mindset can make a huge difference in managing anxiety, and I'll dive into the power of gratitude as a tool for shifting your focus from fear to peace.

How Your Mindset Impacts Anxiety

Your mind is a powerful tool, and the way you think shapes your experience of the world. When you're stuck in negative thinking patterns, it can feel like anxiety takes control. Thoughts like *"What if something bad happens?"* or *"I'm not good enough"* add fuel to the fire, making anxiety worse.

This doesn't mean that anxiety is all "in your head" or that you can just think your way out of it. But changing the way you think can help reduce anxious feelings over time. Think of your mindset as the lens through which you view life. If your lens is clouded with negativity, everything seems more stressful. But when you clear that lens by focusing on more positive and hopeful thoughts, life can feel lighter and less overwhelming.

One of the most effective ways to manage anxiety is to challenge your negative thoughts. Here are some simple ways to shift your thinking when anxiety starts to creep in:

1. Replace "What If" with "What Is"

Anxiety often comes from worrying about what *might* happen. You may find yourself thinking, *"What if I mess up?"* or *"What if things go wrong?"* Instead of focusing on the unknown future, bring yourself back to the present moment by asking, *"What is happening right now?"* This helps ground you in reality and reduces anxious predictions about the future.

2. Use Positive Self-Talk

When you catch yourself thinking negatively, try replacing those thoughts with more supportive and positive ones. For example, if you're thinking, *"I can't handle this,"* try shifting it to *"I've handled challenges before, and I can do it again."* Positive self-talk helps reduce fear and builds confidence.

3. Focus on What You Can Control

Anxiety often comes from feeling out of control. Instead of worrying about things that are beyond your control, shift your focus to the things you *can* control. For example, you can't control the outcome of every situation, but you can control how you prepare, how you respond, and how much effort you put in.

The Power of Gratitude: How Focusing on the Positive Can Ease Anxiety

Gratitude is one of the simplest yet most powerful tools for easing anxiety. When we're anxious, our minds tend to fixate on what's wrong—what's missing, what could go wrong, or what we wish we had. Gratitude flips this around by encouraging us to focus on what's *right*—what we already have, what's going well, and what we can be thankful for in our lives.

How Gratitude Shifts Your Focus

When you focus on the things you're grateful for, it's like rewiring your brain to see the positives in your life instead of only the negatives. Gratitude helps reduce stress and anxiety because it reminds you of the good things, even in difficult times. It shifts your mind from scarcity (*"I don't have enough"*) to abundance (*"I already have so much to be thankful for"*).

Focusing on gratitude also helps reduce fear, which is often at the heart of anxiety. When you're anxious, you might fear losing something important—your health, job, relationships, or sense of security. Gratitude helps calm these fears by reminding you of the blessings and strengths you already have in your life.

Daily Gratitude Practices to Improve Your Mood and Outlook

Gratitude is more than just a nice idea—it's something you can practice daily to improve your mental health. Here are some simple gratitude practices that can help ease anxiety and brighten your outlook:

1. Keep a Gratitude Journal

Every day, take a few minutes to write down three things you're grateful for. These don't have to be big things—sometimes the smallest things, like a warm cup of coffee or a kind word from a friend, can have the biggest impact. By consistently practicing gratitude, you train your mind to notice the positives more easily.

2. Start Your Day with Gratitude

Before you even get out of bed in the morning, think of one thing you're thankful for. It could be something simple, like waking up rested, having a roof over your head, or looking forward to something that day. Starting your day with gratitude sets a positive tone and helps keep anxiety at bay.

3. Use Gratitude as a Grounding Technique

When anxiety hits, it can be hard to calm your racing thoughts. One way to ground yourself is by mentally listing things you're grateful for. You can focus on your surroundings, like the comfort of your home, or on bigger things, like the support of loved ones. This simple exercise helps shift your mind away from anxious thoughts and back to a place of peace.

4. Express Gratitude to Others

Another way to practice gratitude is by expressing it to the people around you. Send a text to a friend, family member, or coworker thanking them for something they've done. Not only does this strengthen your relationships, but it also boosts your own sense of well-being.

The power of positive thinking and gratitude can't be overstated when it comes to managing anxiety. By shifting your mindset and focusing on the good, you create a mental space that is less welcoming to fear and anxiety. Remember, while it's natural to have anxious thoughts from time to time, you can take control of your mind by replacing negativity with positivity and gratitude.

Incorporating these practices into your daily life won't eliminate anxiety overnight, but with consistency, you'll notice a shift in how you handle stress and challenges. Gratitude helps you see life through a brighter lens, and positive thinking empowers you to face anxiety with calm and confidence.

"You have the power to choose how you respond to stress. Breathe, reset, and keep moving forward."

CHAPTER 7

Building a Support System – You Don't Have to Do It Alone

One of the most difficult things about anxiety is feeling like you have to face it on your own. The truth is, you don't. Reaching out to others for support can be one of the most effective ways to manage anxiety. Whether it's talking to friends and family or seeking help from professionals, knowing that you have people on your side can make a huge difference.

In this chapter, I'll explore the importance of building a support system, how to ask for help without feeling like a burden, the value of support groups, and how therapy—especially Cognitive

Behavioral Therapy (CBT)—can help you manage your anxiety more effectively.

The Importance of Talking to Someone: Friends, Family, or Professionals

When you're dealing with anxiety, it can be easy to bottle up your feelings. You may think, *"I don't want to bother anyone with my problems,"* or *"Nobody will understand what I'm going through."* However, talking to someone you trust is one of the most effective ways to release anxiety. Sharing your thoughts and feelings can lighten the emotional load and provide a fresh perspective.

Friends and Family

Your friends and family care about you, and many of them would be happy to support you.

Sometimes, just having someone listen without judgment can ease anxiety. It's okay if you don't have all the answers or if you're unsure how to explain what you're feeling. Opening up is the first step. You don't need to have a solution; you just need someone to share the weight.

Professionals

If your anxiety feels overwhelming or constant, it might be time to talk to a professional. Therapists, counselors, and mental health professionals are trained to help you understand and manage anxiety in a healthy way. Reaching out for professional help is not a sign of weakness—it's a sign of strength. Sometimes, you need extra support to navigate the challenges of anxiety, and that's completely okay.

How to Ask for Help Without Feeling Like a Burden

It's common to worry about being a burden when asking for help. You might think that your problems aren't "big enough" to bother others, or you might feel guilty for leaning on someone. These thoughts can prevent you from reaching out, but they're not true. Here's how you can ask for help in a way that feels comfortable:

1. Be Honest and Direct

When you're struggling, be honest about how you're feeling. You can say something like, *"I've been feeling really anxious lately, and I could use someone to talk to."* Being direct helps the other person understand how they can support you.

2. Ask for Specific Support

Sometimes, people don't know how to help unless you tell them. If you need someone to listen, say so. If you need advice or a distraction, let them know. By being clear about what you need, you make it easier for others to offer the right kind of help.

3. Understand That People Care

Remind yourself that asking for help doesn't make you a burden. People who care about you *want* to help. Think about how you would feel if a loved one came to you for support—you wouldn't think of them as a burden. The same applies to you.

Support Groups: What They Are, and How to Find One That Suits You

Support groups are a great way to connect with others who understand what you're going through. These groups are designed to bring together people facing similar challenges, and they provide a safe space to share experiences, give and receive advice, and offer emotional support.

What Is a Support Group?

A support group is typically led by a facilitator (sometimes a mental health professional) and involves group discussions where members share their experiences with anxiety or related struggles. The goal is to help each other feel understood, reduce feelings of isolation, and offer practical tips for coping.

How to Find a Support Group

There are many ways to find a support group. You can start by asking your doctor or therapist for recommendations. You can also search online for local or virtual groups that focus on anxiety. Websites like *Mental Health America* or *Anxiety and Depression Association of America (ADAA)* often list resources for finding support groups. Whether in person or online, finding the right group can make a significant difference.

Benefits of Joining a Support Group

Support groups offer a unique sense of community. When you're surrounded by people who understand what you're going through, you feel less alone. It can be comforting to know that others face similar challenges, and hearing how they manage anxiety can inspire you to try new strategies.

The Role of Therapy: Cognitive Behavioral Therapy (CBT) and Other Helpful Approaches

Therapy is one of the most effective long-term solutions for managing anxiety. Many forms of therapy can help, but Cognitive Behavioral Therapy (CBT) is especially known for its success in treating anxiety.

What Is Cognitive Behavioral Therapy (CBT)?

CBT is a type of therapy that focuses on changing the negative thought patterns that contribute to anxiety. It teaches you to recognize unhelpful thoughts (like *"I can't do this"* or *"Something bad will happen"*) and replace them with more balanced, realistic ones. By changing how you think, you can change how you feel and act.

CBT also involves learning practical coping skills for managing anxiety in the moment. Over time, these skills can help you reduce the intensity and frequency of anxious feelings.

Other Types of Therapy

Aside from CBT, there are other forms of therapy that might help with anxiety:

- **Mindfulness-Based Therapy:** This approach combines mindfulness practices with traditional therapy to help you stay grounded in the present moment, reducing anxiety about the future.

- **Exposure Therapy**: This involves gradually exposing yourself to the things you fear in a controlled environment, helping you build confidence and reduce avoidance behaviors.

- **Dialectical Behavior Therapy (DBT)**: DBT focuses on teaching emotional regulation skills, which can be especially helpful if anxiety feels overwhelming.

How to Find the Right Therapist

If you're considering therapy, it's important to find a therapist who specializes in anxiety and uses an approach that feels right for you. You can start by asking for recommendations from your doctor or looking for licensed professionals in your area. Online therapy platforms like *BetterHelp* or

Talkspace are also great options if you prefer virtual sessions.

Anxiety can feel isolating, but the truth is, you don't have to face it by yourself. Whether it's opening up to friends and family, joining a support group, or seeking professional therapy, building a strong support system can make all the difference in managing anxiety.

Remember, it's okay to ask for help. Everyone needs support sometimes, and there's strength in reaching out. With the right people by your side, you'll find that anxiety becomes easier to manage, and the peace and calm you're looking for will feel much more within reach.

"*Even when things feel
overwhelming, remember:
you've faced challenges before
and come out stronger.*"

CHAPTER 8

Dealing with Setbacks and Staying on Track

Managing anxiety isn't a one-time fix—it's a journey. Along the way, you might face setbacks, and that's completely normal. Life is unpredictable, and there will be moments when anxiety returns, no matter how much progress you've made. The key is to understand that setbacks are part of the process, not a failure. It's what you do after those setbacks that truly matters.

In this chapter, I'll talk about accepting setbacks, how to pick yourself up when anxiety comes back, and ways to build a personal "toolkit" to help you stay on track during tough times. Finally, I'll discuss long-term strategies for keeping peace and balance in your life, even when things get busy or overwhelming.

Accepting That Setbacks Are Part of the Process, Not a Failure

When you've been doing well managing your anxiety, having a setback can feel discouraging. You might think, *"Why is this happening again? I thought I was getting better."* But it's important to remember that setbacks are not a sign of failure—they are simply part of the journey. No one's path to managing anxiety is perfectly smooth.

Life is full of stressors, both big and small. Sometimes, these stressors can cause your anxiety to spike, even if you've been doing everything right. This doesn't mean you're back to square one, and it certainly doesn't mean you've failed. Setbacks are opportunities to learn more about yourself and what triggers your anxiety. They give you the chance to refine your coping strategies and strengthen your resilience.

How to Pick Yourself Back Up When Anxiety Returns

When anxiety returns, it's easy to fall into a cycle of self-criticism. You might blame yourself for feeling anxious again or think that all the progress you've made is lost. But the first thing you need to do when anxiety comes back is to show yourself some compassion.

1. Acknowledge What You're Feeling

The first step in picking yourself back up is acknowledging that you're feeling anxious. Don't try to push the feelings away or pretend they're not there. Accepting that anxiety has returned is the first step toward managing it.

2. Revisit What Worked in the Past

Think about the tools and strategies that helped you manage anxiety before. Did deep breathing exercises calm you down? Did journaling help you process your thoughts? Going back to what worked in the past can help you regain control when anxiety reappears.

3. Take One Step at a Time

When anxiety comes back, it can feel overwhelming. Instead of trying to tackle everything at once, focus on small, manageable steps. What's one thing you can do right now to ease your anxiety, even if it's something simple like taking a walk or practicing a grounding exercise? Small steps add up, and they'll help you feel more in control.

Creating a Personal "Toolkit" to Manage Anxiety During Difficult Times

One of the best ways to prepare for future setbacks is to create a personal "toolkit" of anxiety management strategies. This toolkit is a collection of coping mechanisms, techniques, and resources that you can turn to when anxiety strikes. The idea is to have a set of go-to tools ready so that you don't feel lost when anxiety returns.

Here are some items you might include in your personal anxiety toolkit:

1. Breathing Techniques

Having a few simple breathing exercises in your toolkit can help calm you down quickly when anxiety hits. Whether it's box breathing (inhale for 4 seconds, hold for 4 seconds, exhale for 4 seconds, and hold for 4 seconds) or the 4-7-8 method (inhale for 4 seconds, hold for 7, exhale for 8), these exercises can be done anywhere, anytime.

2. Grounding Exercises

When you're feeling anxious, grounding techniques can help you stay connected to the present moment. One effective exercise is the "5-4-3-2-1" method: name 5 things you can see, 4 things you can feel, 3 things you can hear, 2 things you can smell, and 1 thing you can taste. It helps you shift your focus away from anxious thoughts and onto your surroundings.

3. Self-Soothing Activities

Having a list of self-soothing activities can be a great way to comfort yourself when anxiety flares up. This could include taking a warm bath, listening to calming music, drinking a cup of tea, or practicing meditation. Choose activities that bring you comfort and peace.

4. A Journal

Journaling is a powerful tool for managing anxiety. Writing down your thoughts and feelings can help you process what's going on in your mind. Your journal doesn't have to be fancy—just a place where you can express yourself freely. You can also use it to track your triggers and identify patterns in your anxiety.

5. A List of Support Contacts

Sometimes, you just need to talk to someone. Having a list of friends, family members, or professionals you can reach out to when anxiety hits is important. Don't hesitate to reach out when you need support—that's what your network is for.

Long-Term Strategies for Maintaining Peace and Balance in a Busy World

While quick fixes and coping tools are essential, long-term strategies are just as important for keeping anxiety in check over time. These strategies help create a solid foundation that makes it easier to manage anxiety before it escalates.

1. Establish a Daily Routine

Having a consistent daily routine can provide a sense of stability and reduce anxiety. Whether it's a morning ritual that includes meditation or an evening wind-down routine that helps you relax, creating structure in your day can help you feel more grounded.

2. Prioritize Self-Care

Self-care is not a luxury—it's a necessity, especially when it comes to managing anxiety. Make time for activities that nourish your mind and body, whether it's exercising, eating well, spending time in nature, or simply taking breaks throughout the day.

3. Practice Mindfulness

Mindfulness is about staying present and aware of your thoughts and feelings without judgment. Regular mindfulness practice can help you catch anxious thoughts before they spiral out of control. Even just a few minutes of mindful breathing or meditation each day can make a big difference.

4. Set Realistic Expectations

Sometimes anxiety is fueled by unrealistic expectations. It's important to set achievable goals and recognize that you don't have to be perfect. Give yourself permission to make mistakes and take things one step at a time.

5. Stay Connected

Remember, you're not alone in your journey with anxiety. Stay connected with friends, family, and your support network. Having strong connections with others can make managing anxiety feel less overwhelming.

Setbacks are a natural part of the journey to managing anxiety, but they don't have to define your progress. With the right mindset, tools, and support, you can move through difficult moments and continue building resilience. Your journey isn't about perfection—it's about progress. By accepting setbacks, creating a personal toolkit, and practicing long-term strategies for peace and balance, you'll find that each day brings you closer to the calm and peace you deserve.

CONCLUSION

You've come a long way in understanding and managing your anxiety. The fact that you've taken the time to learn new tools and techniques shows that you're ready to take control of your anxiety and start living a calmer, more peaceful life. This is a journey—your journey—and it begins right now.

It's important to remember that you have the power to shape how you respond to anxiety. Every breathing exercise, every grounding technique, every moment spent reflecting on your triggers is a step toward reclaiming your peace of mind. Anxiety might still come and go, but now you're equipped with the skills to face it head-on.

Keep Using the Tools You've Learned

The tools and techniques covered in this book aren't just quick fixes—they're long-term solutions that can help you build resilience over time. Whether it's practicing mindfulness, reaching out for support, or making small lifestyle changes like getting better sleep and eating well, these actions add up. Don't be afraid to revisit chapters, try new exercises, and continue developing what works best for you.

Building calm in a busy world takes practice, and there will be times when it feels harder than others. But each time you choose to slow down, breathe, and focus on the present moment, you're training your mind to manage anxiety in healthier, more productive ways. You've got everything you need to continue this work. The more you use these tools, the stronger your ability to handle stress and anxiety will become.

Peace Is Always Within Reach, Even in Busy Times

Life gets busy. There's no way around it. Work, family, and countless other responsibilities will always demand your time and attention. But even in the middle of all that noise, peace is still possible. It's easy to believe that peace can only happen when everything around you is calm, but true peace is found when you learn to stay calm, even when life is hectic.

You've learned techniques to calm your mind no matter where you are—whether it's in a stressful meeting, a crowded event, or just dealing with a full to-do list at home. The key is to keep coming back to the present, to keep practicing what you've learned, and to trust that, with time, your moments of anxiety will feel less overwhelming.

Finding Calm Is a Lifelong Journey, Not a Race

There's no finish line when it comes to managing anxiety. It's a lifelong journey that will evolve and change as you grow. Some days, you might feel completely at peace, while other days might challenge you. That's okay. What matters is that you keep moving forward, taking each day as it comes, and using what you've learned to stay balanced.

The journey to calm isn't about being perfect—it's about being patient with yourself, showing yourself compassion, and continuing to try. Every effort you make to slow down, reflect, and take care of your mind is progress. And with each step you take, you're building a foundation of calm that will support you, no matter what life throws your way.

Your journey to calm has already begun. With the tools and strategies you now have, you're equipped to manage anxiety in ways that will bring more peace into your daily life. Remember, it's not about never feeling anxious again—it's about learning how to respond when those feelings arise, knowing that you have the strength to handle them.

As you move forward, keep reminding yourself that peace and calm are always within reach. You are not alone in this journey, and with time, patience, and practice, you will continue to find more balance and joy in your life.

Take it one step at a time—your journey to calm starts now.